T0129531

SAT & ACT

MATHEMATICAL TOOL SHEETS

A Collection of Mathematical Formulas and Procedures for the SAT and ACT Examinations

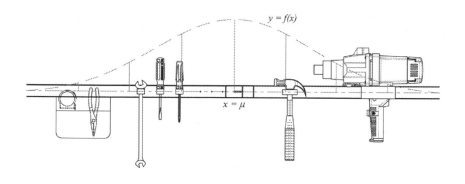

Written by:

Charles Cook

Current Graduate Student and Teaching Assistant - Virginia Tech (Blacksburg, VA)

Former Mathematics Instructor - C2 Education (Westfield & Bridgewater, NJ)

Former Mathematics Tutor - Middlesex County College (Edison, NJ)

© *1st Edition, March 2020*

authorHOUSE®

AuthorHouse™
1663 Liberty Drive
Bloomington, IN 47403
www.authorhouse.com
Phone: 1 (800) 839-8640

Published by AuthorHouse 04/06/2020

ISBN: 978-1-7283-5731-7 (sc)
ISBN: 978-1-7283-5730-0 (e)

Library of Congress Control Number: 2020906463

Print information available on the last page.

Special thanks to:

Stephanie Cook

Mathematics Teacher - Monroe Township High School (Monroe Township, NJ)

&

Edward Helmstetter

Educator - C2 Education (Westfield, NJ)

PREFACE

About

The goal of this guide is to have every mathematical formula and procedure under one roof. This handbook is similar to a formula sheet. It's a collection of formula sheets and instructions on how to use each equation. I call these sheets "tool sheets." A builder needs tools to build his/her house like an engineer needs equations to design and solve problems. This guide can act as your tool belt. Hopefully, it will help build your house, meaning get accepted into college, to begin building the foundation of your future. Throughout the course of studying for the SAT or ACT exam, this guide is best used with problem sets and practice tests. I've personally used this guide as a teaching tool with my former students. It has proved to service both the person learning the material as well as the person teaching the material.

Test Breakdowns

- SAT Math
  - Section 3 – No Calculator   20 problems, 25 minutes
  - Section 4 – Calculator   38 problems, 55 minutes

- ACT Math/Science
  - Section 2 – Math   60 problems, 60 minutes (calculator permitted)
  - Section 4 – Science   40 problems, 35 minutes (calculator not permitted)

Choosing Which Exam to Take

As far as math goes, the topics are quite similar. Two major components to consider when deciding on a test is the science section in the ACT and time. The ACT is more time restrictive so if you're a quick problem solver, efficient reader, and good at interpreting descriptions, tables, and graphs, then taking the ACT may be beneficial. The science section is not about understanding science. It's about making sense of new information. I would work through several practice tests, both SAT and ACT, then decide on one and stick to it. Even though the math is similar, you don't want to waste too much time preparing for the wrong exam.

Study Tips

- Practice tests are key.
- When in doubt, draw it out.
- Don't be afraid to learn more advanced topics. The broader knowledge of mathematics you have, the better.
- I would not rely solely on a preparation book. I've found supplementing prep books with text book lessons and problem sets has been beneficial.
- Do not do your work in a work book. Have a designated notebook for your standardized test studying. In most prep books, there's not enough room for calculations. Give yourself plenty of space to work and think.
- In your notebook, take notes on each lesson and highlight key points.
- When studying, unless a problem is a "guess and check" type, do not rely on answer choices. Meaning, do not look at the options while solving the problem. This forces you to write out steps and fully complete each problem. Real-life mathematics does not provide options "A, B, C, and D".
- Unfortunately, time is a component of standardized test taking. When you begin your studies, do not time yourself. First, get used to the material. Then, once you feel comfortable, begin taking a timed practice test once every couple weeks.

- If you don't know something, use your resources and learn it. You have this guide, your textbooks, and the internet (Google, YouTube, Khan Academy, etc.). Embrace the fact that we all know such a limited amount of information and there is a lifetime of learning ahead of us. If we already knew everything, then what would be the point of living.
- Learn to use your graphing calculator. Technology is a major aspect of modern life. Know how to use it to your advantage. Below are useful calculator functions on the TI-83/84 graphing calculator:
  - *Typing Letters:* press "ALPHA" then press any key with a green letter to the top right
  - *Decimals to Fractions:* "MATH" → "ENTER" → "ENTER"
  - *Fractions to Decimals:* "MATH" → "2" → "ENTER"
  - *Reciprocal Trigonometric Functions:* "1" → "÷" → "SIN" or "COS" or "TAN"
  - *Inverse Trigonometric Functions:* "2ND" → "SIN" or "COS" or "TAN"
  - *Permutation:* enter "n" value then press → "MATH" → left arrow key → "2" → enter "r" value → "ENTER"
  - *Combination:* enter "n" value then press → "MATH" → left arrow key → "3" → enter "r" value → "ENTER"

Recommended Materials

SAT Mathematics:
- "The College Panda SAT Math"
- "Barron's Math Workbook for the New SAT"
- "McGraw Hill Education SAT"
- College Board practice tests[1]

ACT Mathematics:
- "Ultimate Guide to the Math ACT"
- "Barron's ACT Math and Science Workbook"
- Crack ACT[2] and Official ACT[3] practice tests

Supplemental Material:
- "A-Plus Notes for Algebra: Algebra 2 and Pre-Calculus" (offers a broad range of algebraic topics, is well organized, and provides straight forward directions)

Additional Materials:
- The Princeton Review books have good practice tests for both the SAT and ACT exams. They have short problem sets but give good descriptions and summaries of topics.

Links:

[1]https://collegereadiness.collegeboard.org/sat/practice/full-length-practice-tests

[2]http://www.crackact.com/act/

[3]http://www.collegeprepresults.com/official-act-practice-tests-free/

TABLE OF CONTENTS

ADVANCED TOPICS

FOUNDATIONS

DEFINITIONS

Real Number   All rational and irrational numbers.

Integer   A whole number that can be positive, negative, or zero; $\{\cdots, -1, 0, 1, \cdots\}$

          Ex. $-2, 3, 0$.

Rational Number   A number produced by the division of two integers.

          Ex. $\frac{1}{3}, 0.\overline{3}, 0.5, -4, 0$.

Irrational Number   A number that cannot be expressed as the ratio of two integers. Irrational numbers have an infinite number of decimal digits.

          Ex. $\pi, e, \sqrt{2}$

Whole Number   Any positive integer including zero; $\{0, 1, 2, 3, \cdots\}$.

Natural Number   Any positive integer not including zero; $\{1, 2, 3, \cdots\}$.

Imaginary Number   A number expressed in terms of the square root of negative one;

          Ex. $2\sqrt{-1} = 2i$.

Complex Number   A number expressed in terms of both a real and imaginary number;

          Ex. $3 + 2\sqrt{-1} = 3 + 2i$.

Constant   A quantity that does not change. Constants can be represented as a number or letter.

          Ex. $1, 2, a, b$.

Variable   A letter used to represent a single number or a set of numbers that are unknown; Ex. x, y.

Term   A combination of constants and variables being multiplied and/or divided; Ex. $2ax, 3by^2$.

Like Terms   Two or more terms that consist of the same variable(s) with equivalent exponents.

          Ex. $(x + y^2) + (2x + 4y^2) = (x + 2x) + (y^2 + 4y^2) = 3x + 5y^2$

          The different terms are x and y^2. The like terms are x and $2x$ along with y^2 and $4y^2$.

Coefficient   A constant multiplied to a term. Coefficients show reader the amount of like terms;

          Ex. $2x$.

Expression   The sum of a set of terms;

          Ex. $2ax + 3by^2 - 1$.

Relationship Sign   Sign used to form a relationship amongst two expressions.

- Equality Sign: relates two equal expressions; $=$
- Inequality Sign: relates two equal/unequal expressions; $<, \leq, <, \geq$

Equation   Shows the relationship between expressions.

          Ex. 1) $y = x^2 - a$ (Equality Equation)

Ex. 2) $y > x + 1$ (Inequality Equation)

Function   Mathematical equation that defines the independent and dependent variables.

Ex. 1)   if: $y = x^3 - 1$ $\Rightarrow$ then: $y = f(x)$

This example defines y as a function of x where y is the dependent variable and x is the independent variable. Hence, y depends on x, therefore, y is a function of x. In terms of computing, x refers to the input and y refers to the output where the output is dependent upon the input.

Ex. 2)   if: $q = x - 2yt$ $\Rightarrow$ then: $q = f(x, y, t)$

This example defines q as a function of x, y, and t thus forming a multivariable equation with multiple inputs linked to one output.

Function Transformations

Vertical Translation

$$g(x) = f(x) \pm c$$ Shift in direction of constant.

Horizontal Translation

$$g(x) = f(x \pm c)$$ Shift in direction of negative constant.

Vertical Reflection

$$g(x) = f(-x)$$ Negative 1 multiplied directly to x.

Horizontal Reflection

$$g(x) = -f(x)$$ Negative 1 multiplied to entire function.

Vertical Factor

$$g(x) = cf(x)$$ Constant multiplied to entire function.

Horizontal Factor

$$g(x) = f(cx)$$ Constant multiplied directly to x.

	Vertical	Horizontal
$c > 1$	Expansion	Compression
$0 > c > 1$	Compression	Expansion

Function Composition

$$f(x) \circ g(x) = f(g(x))$$ The function g into the function f.

Points   A point is a number or coordinate (collection of numbers) that describes the amount of change in each specified direction. Geometrically, a singular point does not exist because a quantity x, is the change in distance between 0 and x, which is one-dimensional and creates a line. Try to visualize an infinitely small "point. This "point" will grow smaller and smaller, but never equal zero because we cannot visualize zero. Zero is a concept constructed as a point of reference.

Lines   A line is the 1-directional distance between zero and a number; $x = \sqrt{c^2 + 0^2} = c$

Curves A curve is the 2-directional distance between two points along a plane.

- o Linear curve (y changes at a constant rate between consecutive values of x)
- o Non-linear curve (y changes at a varied rate between consecutive values of x)

Connecting the Dots A line is a collection of points (or numbers), a curve is a collection of lines, planes are a collection of curves, objects are a collection of planes, and time is the collection of objects.

Visualization

$x = c$ Point (1-directional) viewed along a line

$y = f(x)$ Curve (2-directional) viewed along a plane

$z = f(x, y)$ Plane (3-directional) viewed in space

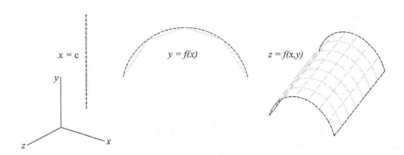

READING & INTERPRETING MATHEMATICS

Throughout this guide, italicized letters generally represent variables (besides the imaginary number) and upright letters represent constants. In descriptions, variables will stand out to the eyes by italicization and constants will be found in quotes. Below is a list explaining some some mathematical notations commonly used. Left to right is the mathematical notation and pronunciation.

Notation	Pronunciation
$f(x)$	f of x **or** f as a function of x
$f(x) = \{u | (a, b)\}$	f of x is equal to u on the interval "a" to "b"
$a_n = \begin{cases} a_1 & | i = 1 \\ a_{i-1}r & | i \geq 2 \end{cases}$	"a_n" is equal to "a_1" when "i" equals 1 and equal to "$a_{i-1}r$" when "i" is greater than or equal to 2
$\Rightarrow$	Then **or** resulting in …
$\therefore$	Therefore…
x_{A_1}	x sub "A" sub 1 **or** x "A" 1

$n!$	"n" factorial
$\{a_i\}_{i=1}^n$	The sequence **or** set "a_i" from "i" equals 1 to "n"
Δx	Delta x **or** change in x
$\Delta x / \Delta t$	Change in x with respect to t
%	Percent
①	Equation #1
$\pm$	Plus or minus
$\sqrt[n]{x}$	"nth" root of x
x^n	x to the power "n"
$f(g(x)) = f \circ g(x)$	f of g of x **or** g into f
$\equiv$	Equivalent
$\rightarrow$	Approaches
$\lvert a \rvert$	Magnitude **or** absolute value of "a"
$\log_b(x)$, $\quad \ln(x)$	Log base "b" of x, natural log of x
$\sum_{i=1}^n x_i$, $\quad \prod_{i=1}^n x_i$	Summation of x sub "i" from "i" equals 1 to "n", Factorial of x sub "i" from "i" equals 1 to "n"

Example: for: $f(x) = \{\sqrt{x} \mid x < 0\} \Rightarrow f(x) \rightarrow \infty$ (undefined)

To be read as: "For f of x equal to the square root of x when x is less than zero, then f of x approaches infinity aka f of x is undefined on the given interval."

TRANSLATING LANGUAGE TO MATHEMATICS

Below is a list to be used to help break down word problems into equations. Left to right is the verbal description and mathematical formulation.

Description	Formulation	Description	Formulation
"n" of x	nx	x is "n" percent of y	$x = \dfrac{n\%}{100\%} y$
x for every y	x/y	x is "n" percent greater than y	$x = \left(1 + \dfrac{n\%}{100\%}\right) y$
x per y	x/y	x is "n" percent less than y	$x = \left(1 - \dfrac{n\%}{100\%}\right) y$
"A" to "B"	A/B	x is greater than y	$x > y$
x is y	$x = y$	x is less than y	$x < y$
x is "n" more than y	$x = y + n$	x is greater than or equal to y	$x \geq y$
x is "n" less than y	$x = y - n$	x is less than or equal to y	$x \leq y$
x is "n" times greater than y	$x = ny$		

DIMENSIONAL UNITS

Numbers represent quantities (length, area, time, etc.) which have their own algebraic properties. Below is a list showing how units evolve throughout mathematical operations. Left to right is the description, mathematical operation, and an example.

Description	Operation	Example
Unit Multiplication:	$u^i * u^j = u^{i+j}$	$5\ (ft^2) * 6\ (ft) = 30\ (ft^3)$
Unit Division:	$u^i / u^j = u^{i-j}$	$6\ (in^3) / 2\ (in^2) = 3\ (in)$
Unit Summation:	$u + u = u$	$2\ (ft) + 3\ (ft) = 5\ (ft)$

DIMENSIONAL ANALYSIS

Below are two examples showing steps for dimensional analysis.

Prove: $\quad 1\left(ft/s\right) = 720\ \left(in/min\right)$

Convert: $\quad 1\left(\dfrac{ft^2}{s}\right)$ to $\left(\dfrac{yd^2}{s}\right)$

Step #1:
$$\frac{1\ ft}{s} \xRightarrow{s \to min} \frac{ft}{s} * \frac{60\ s}{1\ min} = \frac{60\ ft}{min}$$

$$\frac{ft^2}{s} \xRightarrow{ft^2 \to yd^2} \frac{ft^2}{s} * \left(\frac{1\ yd}{3\ ft}\right)^2 = \frac{ft^2}{s} * \frac{1^2\ yd^2}{3^2\ ft^2}$$

Step #2:
$$\frac{60\ ft}{min} \xRightarrow{ft \to in} \frac{60\ ft}{min} * \frac{12\ in}{1\ ft} = \frac{720\ in}{min}$$

$$= \frac{1\ yd^2}{9\ s} \approx 0.11 \left(\frac{yd^2}{s}\right)$$

RATIOS

DEFINITIONS

Ratio: Shows how much one quantity is comprised of another quantity. Ratios are fractions and thought of as a part of a whole. When converting from fraction to decimal form, the decimal shows how many parts the ratio is comprised of with respect to 1 unit.

Percentage: Expresses an equivalent ratio of a number x out of 100, compared to another fraction with a denominator other than 100. In other words, a percentage is a ratio with respect to 100 units.

Percent Change: Expresses the increase or decrease from one quantity to another with respect to the initial amount. This is the change in a value expressed as a percentage.

Proportion: Equation showing the relationship between different values. This relationship is shown with the proportionality factor "k".

Proportion Relation: Shows the relation between similar ratios (group "1" versus group "2").

CONSTANTS & VARIABLES

x	ratio (x units out of 1 unit)	$\%\Delta$	percent change ($\uparrow$ if positive, $\downarrow$ if negative)
$x\%$	percentage (x units out of 100 units)	F	final amount
A	partial quantity ("A" units out of "B" units)	I	initial amount
B	total quantity	k	proportionality factor

RATIO EQUATIONS

Left to right is the description, denotation, ratio form, and fraction form.

Description	Denotation	Ratio Form	Fraction Form
Ratio	x	$A : B$	$\dfrac{A}{B} = \dfrac{partial}{total}$
Percentage	$x\%$	$(A : B) * 100\%$	$\dfrac{A}{B} * 100\%$
Percent Change	$\%\Delta$	$\big((F - I) : I\big) * 100\%$	$\dfrac{F - I}{I} * 100\%$
Direct Proportionality	$A = kB$	$(A : B)_1 = (A : B)_2$	$\left(\dfrac{A}{B}\right)_1 = \left(\dfrac{A}{B}\right)_2$
Inverse Proportionality	$A = k/B$	$A_1 : A_2 = B_2 : B_1$	$\dfrac{A_1}{A_2} = \dfrac{B_2}{B_1}$

SINGLE-VARIABLE

ALGEBRA

SOLVE FOR UNKNOWN QUANTITY

Example: $2(x + 1) + 3x - 2 = 6x + 5$

Solve for the variable x. The left side of the equation must be expanded and simplified. The right side is already simplified. Below are steps on how to solve. Left to right are the step numbers, verbal instructions, before, and after steps.

No.	Verbal Instructions	Before	After
1	Distribute any coefficients being multiplied to multiple terms.	$2(x + 1)$	$2x + 2$
2	Combine any like terms on same side of relationship sign.	$2x + 2 + 3x - 2$	$5x$
3	Combine any like terms on opposite sides of relationship sign.	$5x = 6x + 5$ $-6x \quad -6x$	$-1x = 5$
4	Cancel variable coefficient by multiplying or dividing.	$\dfrac{-1x}{-1} = \dfrac{5}{-1}$	$\boxed{x = -5}$

SOLVE FOR VARIABLE

Example: $2(x + t) + 3t - 2 = 6xt + 5$

Solve for x in terms of t hence determine an equation for $x = f(t)$. The left side of the equation must be expanded and simplified. The right side is already simplified. Below are steps on how to solve. Left to right are the verbal instructions, before, and after steps.

No.	Verbal Instructions	Before	After
1	Distribute any coefficients being multiplied to multiple terms.	$2(x + t)$	$2x + 2t$
2	Combine any like terms on same side of relationship sign.	$2x + 2t + 3t - 2$	$2x + 5t - 2$
3	Combine any like terms on opposite sides of relationship sign.	$2x + 5t - 2 = 6xt + 5$ $+2 \qquad +2$	$2x + 5t = 6xt + 7$
4	Move all terms with desired variable to one side of equation and move all other terms to opposite side of equation.	$2x + 5t = 6xt + 7$ $-6xt \quad -5t \; -6xt \qquad -5t$	$2x - 6xt = 7 - 5t$
5	Factor out desired variable.	$\dfrac{2x - 6xt = 7 - 5t}{x \qquad x}$	$x(2 - 6t) = 7 - 5t$
6	Divide both sides by the remaining terms.	$\dfrac{x(2 - 6t) = 7 - 5t}{(2 - 6t)}$	$\boxed{x = \dfrac{7 - 5t}{2 - 6t}}$

TI-83/84 CALCULATOR METHODS

Instructions on Graphically Solving for x, Given y:

1. Press "Y=" then enter equation into "Y_1"
2. In "Y_2" enter value of y
3. Press "GRAPH" to graph the function.
4. To calculate the intersection press "2ND" → "TRACE" → "5"

i. The calculator will ask, "First curve?" → Press "ENTER"
ii. The calculator will ask, "Second curve?" → Press "ENTER"
iii. The calculator will ask, "Guess?" → Move cursor with arrows towards location of intersection then press "ENTER"
iv. The calculator will output the x and y value of the intersection where y will equal the given value of y and x will equal some number, which is the corresponding x value.

Instructions on Numerically Solving for y, Given x:

1. Enter equation in "Y="
2. Press "2ND" → "WINDOW" → set "Indpnt" to "Ask" and "Depend" to "Auto"
3. Press "2ND" → "GRAPH" to create a table of numerical values
4. Enter value of x → "ENTER"
5. The corresponding value of y is located in the "Y1" column

ALGEBRAIC PROPERTIES

Left to right is the description, before, and after steps.

Description	Before	After
Corresponding like-term coefficients	$ax^2 + bx + c = \alpha x^2 + \beta x + \gamma$	$a = \alpha \quad b = \beta \quad c = \gamma$
Squaring multiple terms	$(x + a)^2$	$(x + a)(x + a) = x^2 + 2ax + a^2$
Factoring out	$ax + ay$	$a(x + y)$
Distributing	$a(x + y)$	$ax + ay$
Distribution foiling	$(x + a)(x + b) \Rightarrow \begin{array}{c|cc} & x & a \\ \hline x & xx & ax \\ b & bx & ab \end{array}$	$x^2 + x(a + b) + ab$
Double fractions (1)	$\dfrac{1/a}{b}$	$\dfrac{1}{ab}$
Double fractions (2)	$\dfrac{a}{1/b}$	ab
Fraction decomposition	$\dfrac{a + b}{x}$	$\dfrac{a}{x} + \dfrac{b}{x}$
Fraction reciprocal	$\dfrac{x}{a} = \dfrac{y}{b}$	$\dfrac{a}{x} = \dfrac{b}{y}$
Fraction addition	$\dfrac{x}{a} + \dfrac{y}{b}$	$\dfrac{bx}{ab} + \dfrac{ay}{ab} = \dfrac{bx + ay}{ab}$

MULTI-VARIABLE

ALGEBRA

SUBSTITUTION METHOD

Example: Equation ①: $2x + 3y = 9$, Equation ②: $-x + 2y = 4$

Note that order of solving for x and y does not matter. One can solve for y first then x and vice versa. Below are steps on how to solve. Left to right are the step numbers, verbal instructions, equation number, before, and after steps.

No.	Verbal Instructions	Equ. No.	Before	After
1	Isolate / solve for $y(x)$ in equation #1	①	$2x + 3y = 9$	$y = 3 - \dfrac{2}{3}x$
2	Plug $y(x)$ into equation #2	②	$-x + 2y = 4$	$-x + 2\left(3 - \dfrac{2}{3}x\right) = 4$
3	Simplify and solve for x	②	$6 - \dfrac{7}{3}x = 4$	$\boxed{x = \dfrac{6}{7}}$
4	Plug the obtained value of x into either equation #1 or #2 and solve for y	①	$2\left(\dfrac{6}{7}\right) + 3y = 9$	$\boxed{y = \dfrac{17}{7}}$

ELIMINATION METHOD

Example: Equation #1: ① $2x + 3y = 9$, Equation #2: ② $-x + 2y = 4$

Note that order of solving for x and y does not matter. One can solve for y first then x and vice versa. Below are steps on how to solve. Left to right are the step numbers, verbal instructions, before, and after steps.

No.	Verbal Instructions	Before/After	
1	Line up x, y, and constant terms	① $2x + 3y = 9$ ② $-x + 2y = 4$	
2	Multiply equation #2 by 2 to get the term, "$-x$" to equal "$-2x$"	$2x + 3y = 9$ $2(-x + 2y) = 2(4)$	
3	Sum terms into one equation	$\begin{array}{rrr} +2x & +3y & = 9 \\ -2x & +4y & = 8 \\ \hline 0x & +7y & = 17 \end{array}$	
4	Solve for the variable, y	$7y = 17$	$\boxed{y = \dfrac{17}{7}}$
5	Plug y into either equation #1 or #2 and solve for x	$2x + 3\left(\dfrac{17}{7}\right) = 9$	$\boxed{x = \dfrac{6}{7}}$

TI-83/84 CALCULATOR METHODS

Instructions on Graphically Solving a System of Equations:

1. Line up equations by hand.

$$a_1x + b_1y + c_1z = d_1$$
$$a_2x + b_2y + c_2z = d_2$$
$$a_3x + b_3y + c_3z = d_3$$

2. In calculator, press "APPS" → "9: PlySmlt2" → "ENTER" → "2: SIMULT EQN SOLVER"
3. Adjust the number of equations and unknowns then push "GRAPH" for "NEXT"
4. Enter coefficients and push "GRAPH" for "SOLVE"
5. x, y, and z will equal "x_1, x_2, and x_3" respectively

Solving Systems of Equations Graphically:

If equations are not given in function form, by hand, isolate the dependent variable y in terms of the independent variable x.

1. Press "Y=" then enter equations into "Y_1" and "Y_2":

$$Y1: \ m_1 x + b_1$$
$$Y2: \ m_2 x + b_2$$

2. Press "GRAPH" to graph the function.
3. To calculate a solution press "2ND" → "TRACE" → "5"
   - i. The calculator will ask, "First curve?" → Press "ENTER"
   - ii. The calculator will ask, "Second curve?" → Press "ENTER"
   - iii. The calculator will ask, "Guess?" → Move cursor with arrows towards location of intersection then press "ENTER"
   - iv. The calculator will output the x and y value of the intersection which is a solution to the system of equations.

SOLUTION TYPES

If equivalent expressions are equal to the same value then we have two of the same equations where there will be an infinite amount of solutions. If equivalent expressions equal different values then there are zero solutions.

$$\text{for: } \begin{cases} ax + by = c \\ \alpha x + \beta y = \gamma \end{cases}, \quad \text{where: } \begin{cases} a = \alpha \\ b = \beta \end{cases} \Rightarrow \quad \begin{array}{l} \text{for: } c = \gamma \Rightarrow \infty \text{ solutions} \\ \text{for: } c \neq \gamma \Rightarrow 0 \text{ solutions} \end{array}$$

LINEAR

FUNCTIONS

GENERAL FORM	SLOPE-INTERCEPT FORM	POINT SLOPE FORM
$ax + by = c$	$y = f(x) = mx + b$	$y - y_1 = m(x - x_1)$

CONSTANTS & VARIABLES

y	dependent variable (function of x)
x	independent variable
m	slope aka rate of change (change in y for every 1 unit change in x)
b	y-intercept which is the initial value of y when $x = 0$
x_1	horizontal distance from origin to point
y_1	vertical distance from origin to point
m_1	slope of "equation 1"
m_2	slope of "equation 2"

GRAPH

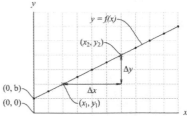

Note that the graph of these functions will show a straight linearly sloped line because the function is defined by a constant rate of change.

TYPES OF SLOPES

Constant Rate of Change:

$$m = \frac{\Delta y}{\Delta x} = \frac{y_2 - y_1}{x_2 - x_1} = \frac{rise}{run}$$

Zero Slope:
(horizontal line) $\quad y = c$

Infinite Slope:
(vertical line) $\quad x = c$

Equal Slopes:
(parallel equations) $\quad m_1 = m_2$

Negative Reciprocal Slopes:
(perpendicular equations) $\quad m_1 = -\dfrac{1}{m_2}$

APPLIED LINEAR EQUATIONS

Left to right is the application, formula, and associated constants and variables.

Application	Formula	Constants & Variables	
Speed	$s = \dfrac{d}{t} = \dfrac{\Delta x}{\Delta t}$	s	change in distance with respect to time
		d	distance
		t	time
Simple Interest	$A(t) = P\left(1 + \dfrac{r\%}{100\%}t\right)$	$A(t)$	total amount of money accumulated over time, t
		t	time in years
		P	initial amount of money
		r	interest rate

ABSOLUTE VALUE FUNCTION

Collection of piecewise functions consisting of multiple equations over specified intervals of x.

Standard Form:
$$f(x) = |x| = \begin{cases} x \mid x \geq 0 \\ -x \mid x \leq 0 \end{cases}$$

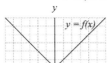

Absolute Equality

$f(x) = |mx + b| \Rightarrow$ ① $f(x) = mx + b$
                    ② $f(x) = -(mx + b)$

Absolute Inequality (note that the inequality sign flips in equation #2)

$f(x) \geq |mx + b| \Rightarrow$ ① $f(x) \geq mx + b$
                    ② $f(x) \leq -(mx + b)$

QUADRATICS

STANDARD FORM

$$y = ax^2 + bx + c$$

discriminant $= b^2 - 4ac$

FACTORED FORM

$$y = (x + m)(x + n)$$

roots: $\begin{matrix} x + m = 0 \\ x + n = 0 \end{matrix}$

VERTEX FORM

$$y = a(x - h)^2 + k$$

vertex $= (h, k)$

CONSTANTS & VARIABLES

h	The x coordinate of the vertex that represents the axis of symmetry.
k	The y coordinate of the vertex that represents the maximum/minimum value of the function.

• Solutions to the quadratic equation give the values of x where the function is equal to zero. This is where the graph crosses the x-axis, which are called x-intercepts (also referred to as roots).
• The discriminant does not produce solutions to the standard quadratic equation but gives information on what kind of solutions the equation will produce;   for: $D > 0 \rightarrow 2$ real   for: $D < 0 \rightarrow$ imaginary.
   for: $D = 0 \rightarrow 1$ real

GRAPH

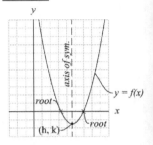

SOLVE BY THE QUADRATIC FORMULA

$$x = \frac{-b \pm \sqrt{b^2 - 4ac}}{2a} \Rightarrow \begin{cases} x_1 = \dfrac{-b + \sqrt{b^2 - 4ac}}{2a} \\ x_2 = \dfrac{-b - \sqrt{b^2 - 4ac}}{2a} \end{cases}$$

Sum: $\quad x_1 + x_2 = -\dfrac{b}{a}$

Product: $\quad x_1 * x_2 = \dfrac{c}{a}$

Vertex: $\quad \left(\dfrac{-b}{2a}, f\left(\dfrac{-b}{2a}\right)\right) = \left(\dfrac{-b}{2a}, c - \dfrac{b^2}{4a}\right)$

SOLVE BY FACTORING (a=1)

Example: $-x - 6 = -x^2$

No.	Verbal Instructions	Before	After
1	Organize equation into standard form.	$-x - 6 = -x^2$	$x^2 - x - 6 = 0$
2	Find two numbers that will add up to the middle term and multiply to the last term.	$(+)(*)$ $x^2 - x - 6 = 0$	$2 - 3 = -1 \quad \checkmark$ $(2)(-3) = -6 \quad \checkmark$
3	Re-write equation into factored form.	$x^2 - x - 6 = 0$	$(x + 2)(x - 3) = 0$
4	Set each factor equal to zero and solve for x.	$x + 2 = 0$ $x - 3 = 0$	$\boxed{x = -2} \Rightarrow \boxed{(-2,0)}$ $\boxed{x = 3} \Rightarrow (3,0)$

FACTORING BY GROUPING (|a| > 1)

Example: $-5x - 2 = -3x^2$

No.	Verbal Instructions	Before	After
1	Organize equation into standard form.	$-5x - 2 = -3x^2$	$3x^2 - 5x - 2 = 0$ $(ax^2 + bx + c = 0)$
2	Multiply "a" and "c" and note "b".	$\underline{3x^2} + \underline{(-5)}x + \underline{(-2)} = 0$	$\underline{ac} = (3)(-2) = -6$ $\underline{\underline{b}} = -5$

3	Find two numbers that will add up to the "b" term and multiply to the "ac" term.	$\underline{ac} = -6\ (*)$ $\underline{b} = -5\ (+)$	$(-6)(1) = -6$ ✓ $1 - 6 = -5$ ✓
4	In quadratic equation, replace "b" term with two numbers calculated in the previous step.	$3x^2 - 5x - 2 = 0$	$(3x^2 - 6x) + (x - 2) = 0$
5	Factor out common constants and variables (4 terms to 2 terms).	$(3x^2 - 6x) + (x - 2) = 0$	$3x(x - 2) + (x - 2) = 0$
6	Repeat step #5 (2 terms to 1 term).	$3x(x - 2) + (x - 2) = 0$	$(x - 2)(3x + 1) = 0$
7	Set each factor equal to zero and solve for x.	$x - 2 = 0$ $3x + 1 = 0$	$\boxed{\begin{array}{l} x = 2 \\ x = -\dfrac{1}{3} \end{array}} \Rightarrow \boxed{\begin{array}{l} (2,0) \\ \left(-\dfrac{1}{3}, 0\right) \end{array}}$

COMPLETING THE SQUARE

Example: $-4x - 6 = -x^2$

No.	Verbal Instructions	Before	After
1	Organize equation into standard form.	$-4x - 6 = -x^2$	$x^2 - 4x - 6 = 0$
2	Bring "c" term to opposite side of equation.	$x^2 - 4x - 6 = 0$	$x^2 - 4x = 6$
3	Calculate the "square".	$\text{square} = \left(\dfrac{b}{2}\right)^2$	$\left(\dfrac{-4}{2}\right)^2 = 4$
4	Add the "square" to both sides of equation.	$x^2 - 4x = 6$	$x^2 - 4x + 4 = 10$
5	Rewrite quadratic equation in factored form.	$x^2 - 4x + 4 = 10$	$(x - 2)^2 = 10$
6	Take square root of both sides of equation.	$(x - 2)^2 = 10$	$\sqrt{(x - 2)^2} = \pm\sqrt{10}$
7	Algebraically solve for x	$x - 2 = \pm\sqrt{10}$	$\boxed{\begin{array}{l} x = \sqrt{10} + 2 \\ x = -\sqrt{10} + 2 \end{array}} \Rightarrow \boxed{\begin{array}{l} (5.16, 0) \\ (-1.16, 0) \end{array}}$

TI-83/84 CALCULATOR METHODS

Graphically Calculating X-Intercepts:

1. Press "Y=" then enter equation into "Y_1"
2. In "Y_2" enter "0"
3. Press "GRAPH" to graph the function.
4. To calculate an x-intercept press "2ND" → "TRACE" → "5"
   - v.   The calculator will ask, "First curve?" → Press "ENTER"
   - vi.   The calculator will ask, "Second curve?" → Press "ENTER"
   - vii. The calculator will ask, "Guess?" → Move cursor with arrows towards location of the x-intercept then press "ENTER"
   - viii. The calculator will output the x and y value of the intersection where y will equal 0 and x will equal some number, which is the x-intercept.

How to Program the Quadratic Formula:

In the edit screen when you're finished, your program should look like following:

PROGRAM: QUAD

:Prompt A, B, C

$:(-B+\sqrt{(B^2-4AC)})/(2A)\rightarrow X$

$:(-B-\sqrt{(B^2-4AC)})/(2A)\rightarrow Y$

:Disp X, Y

1. Create New Program:
   - "PRGM" → "NEW" → Enter "QUAD" (with "ALPHA" green letters)

2. Edit Program:
   - First Line: "PRGM" → "EDIT" → "2ND" → "0" (for "CATALOG") → "Prompt" (press "8" for "P" to shortcut list) → enter "A, B, C" (The first line should appear as "Prompt A, B, C")
   - Second Line: Enter equation with positive square root then press "STO" (bottom left) then "X" (upper left)
   - Third Line: Enter equation with negative square root then press "STO" (bottom left) then "ALPHA" → "1" for "Y"
   - Fourth Line: "2ND" → "0" (for "CATALOG") → "Disp" (press "x^{-1}" for "D" to shortcut list) → enter "X, Y"

3. Deploy program:
   - "PRGM" → "EXEC" → "ENTER" → enter constants a, b, and c then the program will output the solutions to a quadratic equation using the quadratic formula

Instructions on Finding the Vertex of a Quadratic Equation:

1. Press "Y=" then enter equation into "Y_1"
2. Press "GRAPH" to graph the function.
3. To calculate the vertex press "2ND" → "TRACE" → ....
   - If the vertex is a minimum value, press "3"
   - If the vertex is a maximum value, press "4"
   i. The calculator will ask, "Left Bound?" → move cursor to the left side of the vertex then press "ENTER"
   ii. The calculator will ask, "Right Bound?" → move cursor to the right side of the vertex then press "ENTER"
   iii. The calculator will ask, "Guess?" → move cursor to the approximate location of the vertex then press "ENTER"
   iv. The calculator will output the *x* and *y* value of the vertex

EXPONENTIALS

&

LOGARITHMS

EXPONENT PROPERTIES

The square	$x^2 = (-x)^2$
The cube	$x^3 = -(-x)^3$
Adding like terms	$c_1 x^a + c_2 x^a = (c_1 + c_2)x^a$
Adding unlike terms	$x^a + x^b = x^a + x^b$
Multiplication	$x^a x^b = x^{a+b}$
Division	$x^a / x^b = x^{a-b}$
Double exponent	$\left(x^a y^b\right)^c = x^{ac} y^{bc}$
Equivalent base theorem	if: $\quad a^x = a^y$ then: $x = y$
Zero power	$x^0 = 1$
Negative 1	$(-1)^n = \begin{cases} -1, \text{if n is odd} \\ 1, \text{if n is even} \end{cases}$

RADICAL PROPERTIES

The square root	$\sqrt{x} = \sqrt[2]{x} = \pm x^{\frac{1}{2}}$
The cube root	$\sqrt[3]{x} = x^{\frac{1}{3}}$
Adding like terms	$c_1 \sqrt{x} + c_2 \sqrt{x} = (c_1 + c_2)\sqrt{x}$
Adding unlike terms	$\sqrt[a]{x} + \sqrt[b]{x} = \sqrt[a]{x} + \sqrt[b]{x}$
Multiplication	$\sqrt{xt} = \sqrt{x} * \sqrt{t}$
Division	$\sqrt{x/t} = \sqrt{x}/\sqrt{t}$
Double radical	$\sqrt[b]{\sqrt[a]{x}} = \left(x^{1/a}\right)^{1/b} = x^{1/(ab)}$
Radical to exponent	$\sqrt[a]{x^b} = x^{\frac{b}{a}}$
Rationalization	$\dfrac{1}{\sqrt{x}} = \dfrac{1}{\sqrt{x}\sqrt{x}} \dfrac{\sqrt{x}}{} = \dfrac{\sqrt{x}}{x}$
Undefined	for: $\quad f(x) = \{\sqrt{x} \mid x < 0\}$ then: $f(x) \to \infty$

EXPONENTIAL EQUATIONS

Standard Form: $\quad y = ab^x$

a	coefficient
b	base ($b > 0$, $b \neq 1$) which is the rate of change or growth/decay rate • Exponential decay: $\quad 0 < b < 1$ • Exponential growth: $\quad b > 1$

Compound Interest Formula:

$$A(t) = P\left(1 + \frac{r}{n}\right)^{nt}, \quad \text{if: } n = 1 \Rightarrow A(t) = P(1+r)^t$$

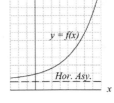

A(t)	total amount of money accumulated over time, t
t	time in years
P	initial amount of money
r	interest rate
n	number of times interest is compounded per year

If compounded annually:	$n = 1$
If compounded semi-annually:	$n = 2$
If compounded quarterly:	$n = 4$
If compounded monthly:	$n = 12$

LOGARITHMIC PROPERTIES

Logarithmic Form:	$y = \log_b(x)$
Exponential Form:	$b^y = x$
Base 10:	$\log(x) = \log_{10}(x)$
Base e:	$\log_e(x) = \ln(x)$
Properties:	$\log(1) = \ln(1) = 0$ $\log_b(b) = 1$ $b^{\log_b(x)} = x$
Exponent:	$\log(x^t) = t\log(x)$

Addition:	$\log(x) + \log(t) = \log(xt)$
Subtraction:	$\log(x) - \log(t) = \log\left(\frac{x}{t}\right)$
Change of Base:	$\log_b(x) = \frac{\log(x)}{\log(b)}$

RATIONAL

EQUATIONS

CONSTANTS AND VARIABLES

f(x)	rational function
p(x)	polynomial function in numerator
q(x)	polynomial function in denominator
(*x* - c)	linear expression in denominator where *x* is a variable and "c" is a constant
R	remainder found by plugging "c" into *p(x)*

REMAINDER THM

Used to find remainder without using synthetic or long division.

$$f(x) = \frac{p(x)}{x - c}$$

$$R = p(c)$$

GRAPH

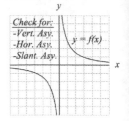

POLYNOMIAL SYNTHETIC DIVISION

Method for simplifying rational expressions with a linear denominator.

Example: $f(x) = \dfrac{3 + 2x^2}{4x + 5}$

No.	Verbal Instructions	Before	After
1	Rearrange numerator from the highest power to the lowest power of *x*, left to right. Use 0 as a place holder if there is a gap in powers between terms.	$\dfrac{3 + 2x^2}{4x + 5}$	$\dfrac{2x^2 + 0x + 3}{4x + 5}$
2	Set denominator equal to 0 and solve for *x*.	$4x + 5 = 0$	$x = -5/4$
3	Set up synthetic division by laying out coefficients in the order that corresponds to the equation in step #1. Bring down the constant "2" under the addition bar.	$\dfrac{2x^2 + 0x + 3}{4x + 5}$	$-5/4 \rfloor \begin{array}{ccc} 2 & 0 & 3 \\ \downarrow & - & - \\ \hline 2 & - & - \end{array}$
4	Multiply "2" and "-5/4". Write result under "0". Next add "0" and "-5/2". Write resulting number "-5/2" under addition bar.	$-5/4 \rfloor \begin{array}{ccc} 2 & 0 & 3 \\ \downarrow & - & - \\ \hline 2 & - & - \end{array}$	$-5/4 \rfloor \begin{array}{ccc} 2 & 0 & 3 \\ \downarrow & -5/2 & - \\ \hline 2 & -5/2 & - \end{array}$
5	Repeat process.	$-5/4 \rfloor \begin{array}{ccc} 2 & 0 & 3 \\ \downarrow & -5/2 & - \\ \hline 2 & -5/2 & - \end{array}$	$-5/4 \rfloor \begin{array}{ccc} 2 & 0 & 3 \\ \downarrow & -5/2 & 25/8 \\ \hline 2 & -5/2 & 49/8 \end{array}$
6	Divide solutions (third row under addition bar) by "4" except for the remainder (far right term under addition bar).	$-5/4 \rfloor \begin{array}{ccc} 2 & 0 & 3 \\ \downarrow & -5/2 & 25/8 \\ \hline 2 & -5/2 & 49/8 \end{array}$	$-5/4 \rfloor \begin{array}{ccc} 2 & 0 & 3 \\ \downarrow & -5/2 & 25/8 \\ \hline \frac{2}{4} & \frac{-5/2}{4} & 49/8 \end{array}$
7	Take bold solutions from step #6 and combine into equation form.	$-5/4 \rfloor \begin{array}{ccc} 2 & 0 & 3 \\ \downarrow & -5/2 & 25/8 \\ \hline \frac{2}{4} & \frac{-5/2}{4} & \mathbf{49/8} \end{array}$	$f(x) = \dfrac{1}{2}x - \dfrac{5}{8} + \dfrac{49}{8(4x + 5)}$ (The remainder is the last term)

PROPERTIES OF RATIONAL EQUATIONS

Verbal Description	Mathematical Property
Undefined Rational Functions:	$f(x) = \dfrac{p(x)}{0} \to \infty$ (undefined)
Relationship between 0 and ∞:	$\dfrac{1}{0} \to \infty$ and $\dfrac{1}{\infty} \to 0$
Asymptotes:	$f(x) = \dfrac{p(x)}{q(x)} = \dfrac{a_n x^n + a_{n-1} x^{n-1} + \cdots + a_1 x^1 + a_0}{b_m x^m + b_{m-1} x^{m-1} + \cdots + b_1 x^1 + b_0}$
Horizontal:	if: $n < m$ $\quad$ HA @ $y = 0$ if: $n = m$ $\quad$ HA @ $y = \dfrac{a_n}{b_m}$ if: $n > m$ $\quad$ HA DNE
Vertical:	set $q(x) = 0$ then solve for x (VA @ $x = c$) • Discontinuity @ $x = c$ if $(x - c)$ is also in numerator • Vertical Asymptote @ $x = c$ if $(x - c)$ is not in numerator
Slant: ($s(x)$ is the slant asymptote equation)	$s(x) = \begin{cases} \text{if } n > m \Rightarrow s(x) = q(x)\overline{)p(x)} \\ \quad \text{if } n \leq m \Rightarrow s(x) \text{ DNE} \end{cases}$

GEOMETRY

OF

CIRCLES

DEFINITIONS

Inscribed: When a geometric object lies within another geometric object, where the inside shape "touches" the outside shape, the inner object is said to be inscribed within the outer object.

Angle: Describes the amount of rotation about an endpoint of a line segment to have the opposite endpoint land at a different location in space.

Arc: The curved distance between two points along a plane about a specified origin. A fraction of the circumference of a circle can be considered an arc. A circular arc has a constant radius where a non-circular arc or hyperbolic arc has a varying radius.

Arc Length: Curved length of arc formed from a line segment, with a specified length, rotated at a specified angle. Can be thought of as circular length.

Arc Degree: Amount of rotation required to form arc (see "central angle for equation").

Chord: Line segment with endpoints that fall along a curve. The diameter of a circle is a chord, but not all chords are diameters.

Inscribed ∠:   An inscribed angle (within a circle) is formed when two chords share the same endpoint along the circle, which is the vertex of the inscribed angle.

Central ∠:   Within a circle, the central angle is the angle formed from two radial chords.

Intcp. ⌢:   The arc formed from the portion of a circle that lies between two chords.

Note: *∠ is the symbol for angle and ⌢ is the symbol for arc.*

CONSTANTS AND VARIABLES

(x_m, y_m):   coordinates of midpoint r: radius of circle

(x_1, y_1):   coordinates of point "1" A_c: area of circle

(x_2, y_2):   coordinates of point "2" π: circumference/diameter ≈ 3.14

d: distance between points s: arc length

(h, k):   center of circle coordinates θ: angle of arc in radians

(x, y):   coordinates of any point on circle C: circumference of circle

GEOMETRICAL RATIOS

Angle Ratio

$$\frac{\text{partial}}{\text{total}} = \frac{\theta}{2\pi} \text{ (radians)} = \frac{\theta}{360°} \text{ (degrees)}$$

Arc Length Ratio (simplifies to angle ratio)

$$\frac{\text{partial}}{\text{total}} = \frac{s}{C} = \frac{r\theta}{2\pi r} = \frac{\theta}{2\pi} \text{ (radians)}$$

Sector Area Ratio (simplifies to angle ratio)

$$\frac{\text{partial}}{\text{total}} = \frac{A_s}{A_c} = \frac{\left(\frac{1}{2}\right)r^2\theta}{\pi r^2} = \frac{\theta}{2\pi} \text{ (radians)}$$

CONVERTING RADIANS AND DEGREES

$$\text{Radians to Degrees} \Rightarrow * \frac{180°}{\pi \text{ rad}} \qquad \text{Degrees to Radians} \Rightarrow * \frac{\pi \text{ rad}}{180°}$$

MIDPOINT FORMULA

Used to find the midpoint coordinate between two points. The midpoint is the average of the horizontal distances and vertical distances between the two points.

$$(x_m, y_m) = \left(\frac{x_1 + x_2}{2}, \frac{y_1 + y_2}{2}\right)$$

DISTANCE FORMULA

Used to find the distance between two points.

$$d = \sqrt{(x_2 - x_1)^2 + (y_2 - y_1)^2}$$

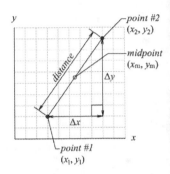

EQUATION OF A CIRCLE

The equation of a circle is the distance formula. This equation models the distance between the center of the circle and any point on that circle.

$$r^2 = (x - h)^2 + (y - k)^2$$

CIRCULAR LENGTH		CIRCULAR AREA	
Arc Length	Circumference	Sector Area	Area of Circle
$s = r\theta$	$C = 2\pi r$	$A_s = \frac{1}{2}r^2\theta$	$A_c = \pi r^2$

Note: θ must be in radians

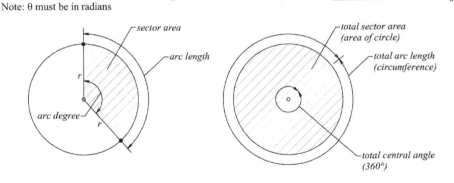

THEOREMS

Relating Arc Degree with the Central Angle

$$arc\ degree = central\ angle$$

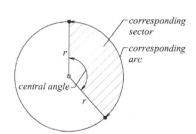

Relating Inscribed and Central Angles (1)
(with common intercepted arcs)

$$inscribed\ angle = \frac{1}{2} * central\ angle$$

*Only applies to inscribed angles that share endpoints (opposite the vertex) with the central angle. The two angles as a result will have the same intercepted arc.

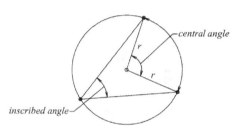

Relating Inscribed and Central Angles (2)
(with common intercepted arcs)

$$inscribed\ angle\ \#1 = inscribed\ angle\ \#2$$

*Only applies to two inscribed angles that share the same endpoints (opposite their vertices). If they share the same endpoints, then they share the same intercepted arc. As a result, the two angles are congruent.

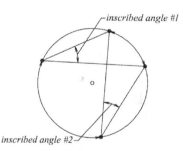

Relating an Inscribed Angle with a Diameter Chord:

$$inscribed\ angle = 90° = \frac{\pi}{2}\ radians$$

*If an inscribed angle shares endpoints (opposite the vertex) with a diameter chord, then the inscribed angle will be right.

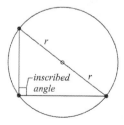

GEOMETRY

OF

TRIANGLES

CONSTANTS AND VARIABLES

A_T: area of triangle

b: length of base of triangle

h: height of triangle

a: side length of equilateral triangle

x_1, y_1: lengths of any two legs on "triangle 1"

x_2, y_2: lengths of corresponding legs on "triangle 2"

a,b,c: leg lengths of opposite angles

n: number of sides/vertices of polygon

AREA OF GENERAL AND EQUILATERAL TRIANGLES

Area of General Triangle: $A_T = \dfrac{1}{2}bh$, Area of Equilateral Triangle: $A_T = \dfrac{\sqrt{3}}{4}a^2$

SPECIAL TRIANGLES

Isosceles Triangle: Two congruent leg lengths where the opposite angles are also congruent.

Equilateral Triangle: All three leg lengths are congruent where the opposite angles are also congruent and equal 60° or π/3.

TRIANGLE INEQUALITY THEOREM

The sum of any two sides of a triangle must be greater than the third side where a, b, and c are the lengths of the triangle legs.

$$a + b > c \qquad a + c > b \qquad b + c > a$$

METHOD OF SIMILAR TRIANGLES

When comparing two different triangles, if they have two corresponding congruent angles, then the triangles are similar. This means that the ratios of their corresponding side lengths will equal.

$$\frac{x_1}{y_1} = \frac{x_2}{y_2}$$

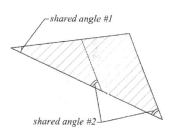

shared angle #1

shared angle #2

LAW OF SINES

The ratio between any side length to the sinusoidal function of its opposite angle is equal to the ratio of any other side length to the sinusoidal function of its opposite angle.

$$\frac{a}{\sin(A°)} = \frac{b}{\sin(B°)} = \frac{c}{\sin(C°)}$$

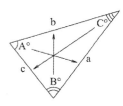

32

LAW OF COSINES

Used when given an angle and the two adjacent leg lengths to calculate the leg length opposite the known angle.

$$c^2 = a^2 + b^2 - 2ab\cos(C°)$$

POLYGON DIAGONAL EQUATION

Used to calculate the number of diagonals within a 2-D polygon.

$$\text{No. of Diagonals} = \frac{n(n-3)}{2}$$

INTERIOR ANGLE SUM FORMULA

Used to calculate the sum of the interior angles of a 2-D polygon.

$$\sum_i \theta_i = 180°(n-2) = \pi(n-2)$$

MISCELLANEOUS GEOMETRICAL DRAWINGS

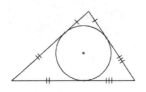

Inscribed Circle within a Triangle
Walk Around (Lengths)

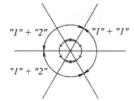

Walk Around (Angles)

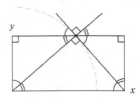

Opposite Angles

TRIGONOMETRY

DEFINITION

Trigonometry is the branch of mathematics that is focused on the study of right triangles. A trigonometric function describes a ratio amongst two different side lengths of a right triangle. These ratios are functions of the angle between the two sides.

CONSTANTS AND VARIABLES

x: length of horizontal leg

y: length of vertical leg (equivalent to height of right triangle)

H: length of hypotenuse (longest side of right triangle, opposite length from right angle)

θ: angle that forms between two different sides of the right triangle

O: opposite side length from angle

A: adjacent side length from angle

H: hypotenuse

P: period

|a|: amplitude (does not exist for tangent and cotangent functions)

b: coefficient being multiplied to θ

SPECIAL RIGHT TRIANGLES

Right Triangle Type	Description	Side Lengths
45°-45°-90°	Two congruent leg lengths	x
	Hypotenuse	$x\sqrt{2}$
30°-60°-90°	Leg adjacent to 30° angle	$x\sqrt{3}$
	Leg adjacent to 60° angle	x
	Hypotenuse	$2x$

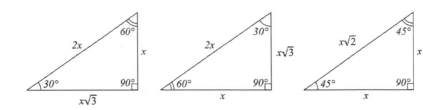

PYTHAGOREAN THEOREM

The Pythagorean Theorem is the distance formula. This equation models the distance between the horizontal and vertical distance at each end of the hypotenuse on the x-y coordinate plane. The hypotenuse is simply a connection between two points.

$$x^2 + y^2 = H^2 \quad \text{(Only applies to right triangles)}$$

TRIGONOMETRIC FUNCTIONS   (SOH CAH TOA)

$$\sin(\theta) = \frac{O}{H} \qquad \cos(\theta) = \frac{A}{H} \qquad \tan(\theta) = \frac{O}{A}$$

$$\csc(\theta) = \frac{H}{O} \qquad \sec(\theta) = \frac{H}{A} \qquad \cot(\theta) = \frac{A}{O}$$

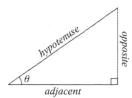

TRIGONOMETRIC IDENTITIES

Reciprocal identity:

$$\sin(\theta) = \frac{1}{\csc(\theta)} \qquad \cos(\theta) = \frac{1}{\sec(\theta)} \qquad \tan(\theta) = \frac{1}{\cot(\theta)}$$

Relating sine and cosine with the tangent:

$$\tan(\theta) = \frac{\sin(\theta)}{\cos(\theta)} \qquad \cot(\theta) = \frac{\cos(\theta)}{\sin(\theta)}$$

Relating sine with the cosine, tangent with the cotangent, and cosecant with the secant:

$$\sin(\theta) = \cos\left(\frac{\pi}{2} - \theta\right) \qquad \tan(\theta) = \cot\left(\frac{\pi}{2} - \theta\right) \qquad \csc(\theta) = \sec\left(\frac{\pi}{2} - \theta\right)$$

Pythagorean identities:

$$\sin^2(\theta) + \cos^2(\theta) = 1 \qquad \tan^2(\theta) + 1 = \sec^2(\theta) \qquad \cot^2(\theta) + 1 = \csc^2(\theta)$$

CORRESPONDING LIKE TRIGONOMETRIC FUNCTIONS

$$\text{if: } \mathrm{trig}(\theta) = \mathrm{trig}(\phi) \Rightarrow \theta = \phi$$

Example:

$$\sin(\theta) = \cos(\phi) \Rightarrow \cos\left(\frac{\pi}{2} - \theta\right) = \cos(\phi) \therefore \frac{\pi}{2} - \theta = \phi$$

INVERSE TRIGONOMETRIC FUNCTIONS

Used to solve for an angle of a trigonometric equation. When an inverse trigonometric function is applied to the trigonometric function itself, they cancel each other and leave remaining the angle, θ.

Example: $\sin(\theta) = n$

1. Apply inverse function to both sides $\sin^{-1}(\sin(\theta)) = \sin^{-1}(n)$
2. Calculate angle with inverse function $\theta = \sin^{-1}(n)$

THE UNIT CIRCLE

The unit circle is a circle graphed on the *x-y* coordinate plane centered at (0, 0) with a radius of 1 unit long. The radius is referred to as the hypotenuse. The angle is measured from the positive *x*-axis; counterclockwise is positive rotation and clockwise is negative rotation. Any point on that circle has an *(x, y)* coordinate which refers to the cosine and sine functions respectively: $(x, y) = (\cos\theta, \sin\theta)$.

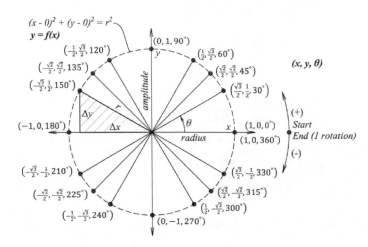

Special Angles in the 1st Quadrant

θ	$\theta°$	$\sin\theta$	$\cos\theta$	$\tan\theta$
0	0°	0	1	0
$\pi/6$	30°	1/2	$\sqrt{3}/2$	$\sqrt{3}/3 = 1/\sqrt{3}$
$\pi/4$	45°	$\sqrt{2}/2 = 1/\sqrt{2}$	$\sqrt{2}/2 = 1/\sqrt{2}$	1
$\pi/3$	60°	$\sqrt{3}/2$	1/2	$\sqrt{3}$
$\pi/2$	90°	1	0	∞

θ	$\theta°$	$\csc\theta$	$\sec\theta$	$\cot\theta$
0	0°	∞	1	∞
$\pi/6$	30°	2	$2/\sqrt{3}$	$3/\sqrt{3} = \sqrt{3}$
$\pi/4$	45°	$2/\sqrt{2} = \sqrt{2}$	$2/\sqrt{2} = \sqrt{2}$	1
$\pi/3$	60°	$2/\sqrt{3}$	2	$1/\sqrt{3}$
$\pi/2$	90°	1	∞	0

Note: $\infty \equiv$ Undefined

WAVE PERIOD AND AMPLITUDE

The period of a trigonometric function describes the angle where the function makes a full rotation. The equation representing the sine function also applies for the cosine, secant, and cosecant. The equation representing the tangent function also applies for the cotangent. The amplitude represents the maximum displacement of the function $f(\theta)$.

$$f(\theta) = a\sin(b\theta) \;\Rightarrow\; P = \frac{2\pi}{b} \qquad f(\theta) = \tan(b\theta) \;\Rightarrow\; P = \frac{\pi}{b}$$

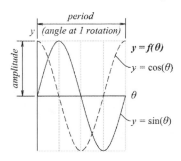

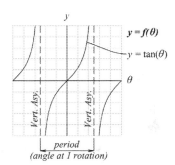

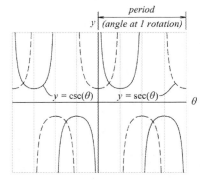

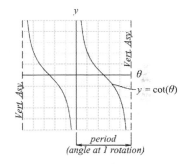

ADVANCED

TOPICS

3-DIMENSIONAL GEOMETRY - GEOMETRIC SOLIDS

	Cylinders	Cones	Pyramids	Spheres
Volume	$\pi r^2 h$	$\dfrac{1}{3}\pi r^2 h$	$\dfrac{1}{3}lwh$	$\dfrac{4}{3}\pi r^3$
Lateral Surface Area	$2\pi rh$	$\pi r\sqrt{r^2 + h^2}$	$2w\sqrt{h^2 + \dfrac{l^2}{4}}$	NA
Surface Area of Base	πr^2	πr^2	lw	NA
Total Surface Area	$2\pi r(h + r)$	$\pi r\left(\sqrt{r^2 + h^2} + r\right)$	$2w\sqrt{h^2 + \dfrac{l^2}{4}} + lw$	$4\pi r^2$

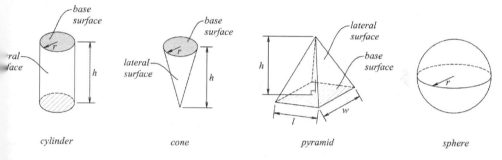

cylinder　　　　　cone　　　　　pyramid　　　　　sphere

COMPLEX NUMBERS

Standard Form:
$$z = a + bi$$

Conjugate Form:
$$z = a - bi$$

Constants and Variables:
- a: real term
- bi: imaginary term
- $|z|$: complex modulus (magnitude or distance from origin)
- c: exponent of i

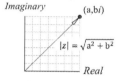

Rationalizing Complex Fractions:

The complex conjugate is used to rationalize a complex rational equation.

$$\frac{1}{a + bi} * \frac{a - bi}{a - bi} = \frac{a - bi}{a^2 - b^2 i^2} = \frac{a - bi}{a^2 + b^2}$$

Complex Modulus:

The complex modulus is the distance from the origin to the point (a, b) mapped on the real-imaginary coordinate plane.

$$|z| = \sqrt{a^2 + b^2}$$

Standard Values of i: $\qquad i = \sqrt{-1} \qquad i^2 = -1 \qquad i^3 = -i \qquad i^4 = 1$

Finding Equivalent Forms of i:

- Divide exponent by 4: $i^c \Rightarrow {}^c/_4 = \mathbb{Z} + \mathbb{R}$
- The remainder gives the exponent of the equivalent form: $i^c = i^R$

  Example: $i^{34} \Rightarrow \dfrac{34}{4} = 8.5 = 8 \text{ R2} \therefore i^{34} = i^2 = -1$

SEQUENCES AND SERIES

Constants and Variables:

i:	index or count
n:	final value of i
a_i:	i^{th} term of sequence (intermediate term)
a_n:	n^{th} term of sequence (desired or final term)
a_1:	1st term of sequence
r:	rate of change, $a_i - a_{i-1} \equiv a_{i+1} - a_i$

Sequence:

set of numbers denoted, $\{a_i\}_{i=1}^n = \{a_1, a_2, a_3, \cdots, a_n\}$

Series:

summation of a sequence, denoted S_n

Summation Notation:

General Summation:
$$\sum_{i=1}^n i = i + (i+1) + (i+2) + \cdots + n = (1 + 2 + 3 + \cdots + n)$$

Sequence Summation:
$$S_n = \sum_{i=1}^n a_i = (a_i + a_{i+1} + a_{i+2} + \cdots + a_n) = (a_1 + a_2 + a_3 + \cdots + a_n)$$

Arithmetic Sequence:

Rate: $\qquad r = a_{i+1} - a_i$

(Linear rate of change)

Sequence Set: $\qquad \{a_i\}_{i=1}^n = \{a_1, (a_2 = a_1 + r), (a_3 = a_2 + r), \cdots, (a_n = a_{n-1} + r \,| n \geq 1)\}$

(Each term is a function of the previous term)

n^{th} term equation: $\qquad a_n = a_1 + (n-1)r \,| i = n$

(The term a_n is a function of the 1st term)

Geometric Sequence:

Rate: $\qquad r = {}^{a_{i+1}}/_{a_i}$

(Nonlinear rate of change)

Sequence Set: $\qquad \{a_i\}_{i=1}^n = \left\{a_1, (a_2 = a_1 r), (a_3 = a_2 r), \cdots, \left(a_n = \begin{cases} a_1 & | i = 1 \\ a_{n-1}r & | i \geq 2 \end{cases}\right)\right\}$

(Each term is a function of the previous term)

n^{th} term equation: $a_n = a_1 r^{n-1} \mid i = n$

(The term a_n is a function of the 1st term)

Arithmetic Series: (summation of an arithmetic sequence)

$$S_n = \sum_{i=1}^{n} a_i = a_1 + \sum_{i=2}^{n} (a_1 + (i-1)r) = \frac{n}{2}(a_1 + a_n) = \frac{n}{2}(2a_1 + (n-1)r)$$

Geometric Series: (summation of a geometric sequence)

$$S_n = \sum_{i=1}^{n} a_i = a_1 \sum_{i=1}^{n} r^{i-1} = a_1 \left(\frac{1 - r^n}{1 - r}\right)$$

MATRICES

A matrix is a set of numbers arranged into rows and columns. A matrix is said to have "n" rows by "m" columns. We denote the size of a matrix as an "n x m" matrix. One area of mathematics where matrices are used is in vector calculus where components of a vector can be arranged into a matrix.

Vector Form: $\vec{v} = \begin{Bmatrix} v_x \\ v_y \\ v_z \end{Bmatrix}$ or $\{v_x \quad v_y \quad v_z\}$ Matrix Form: $[A] = A_{nm} = \begin{bmatrix} A_{11} & A_{12} & A_{13} \\ A_{21} & A_{22} & A_{23} \end{bmatrix}$

A_{nm} is a 2 x 3 matrix. The subscripts "n" and "m" refer to the row and column of each component of the matrix.

Matrix Summation:

Add corresponding components of each matrix: $\begin{bmatrix} a & b \\ c & d \end{bmatrix} + \begin{bmatrix} \alpha & \beta \\ \gamma & \delta \end{bmatrix} = \begin{bmatrix} a+\alpha & b+\beta \\ c+\gamma & d+\delta \end{bmatrix}$

Scalars Multiplied with Matrices:

Multiply scalar, "k" with every component: $k\begin{bmatrix} a & b \\ c & d \end{bmatrix} = \begin{bmatrix} ka & kb \\ kc & kd \end{bmatrix}$

Matrix Multiplication:

When multiplying constants and variables, order does not matter. When multiplying matrices, order does matter. To multiply two matrices, first one must determine if the matrices can be multiplied by analyzing the sizes of each matrix.

Example: $[A][B] = [C]$ Note: $[A][B] \neq [B][A]$

1. Identify sizes of each matrix.
    i. A: matrix "A" of size $\{n_1 \times m_1\} = \{a\}$
    ii. B: matrix "B" of size $\{n_2 \times m_2\} = \{b\}$

2. Correspond the sizes of each matrix in the order in which they are being multiplied. To determine whether the matrices can be multiplied, m_1 and n_2 must equal. If they do not equal, they cannot be multiplied.

$$\{a\}\{b\} = \{n_1 \times m_1\}\{n_2 \times m_2\} \implies m_1 = n_2$$

3. Determine size of resulting matrix. The result of "AB" is matrix "C" of size {c}.

$$\{n_1 \times m_1\}\{n_2 \times m_2\} = \{n_1 \times m_2\} = \{c\}$$

4. Perform the matrix multiplication by multiplying each row in matrix "A" with each corresponding column in matrix "B" then take the sum.

$$[A][B] = \begin{bmatrix} A_{11} & \cdots & A_{1m} \\ \vdots & \ddots & \vdots \\ A_{n1} & \cdots & A_{nm} \end{bmatrix} \begin{bmatrix} B_{11} & \cdots & B_{1m} \\ \vdots & \ddots & \vdots \\ B_{n1} & \cdots & B_{nm} \end{bmatrix} = \begin{bmatrix} \sum_i A_{1i}B_{i1} & \cdots & \sum_i A_{1i}B_{im} \\ \vdots & \ddots & \vdots \\ \sum_i A_{ni}B_{i1} & \cdots & \sum_i A_{ni}B_{im} \end{bmatrix} = [C]$$

In other words:

$$\begin{bmatrix} ① & \rightarrow \\ ② & \rightarrow \\ ③ & \rightarrow \end{bmatrix} \begin{bmatrix} ① & ② & ③ \\ \downarrow & \downarrow & \downarrow \end{bmatrix} = \begin{bmatrix} \sum ①① & \sum ①② & \sum ①③ \\ \sum ②① & \sum ②② & \sum ②③ \\ \sum ③① & \sum ③② & \sum ③③ \end{bmatrix}$$

Example #1: $\begin{bmatrix} a & b & c \\ x & y & z \end{bmatrix} \begin{bmatrix} A & X \\ B & Y \\ C & Z \end{bmatrix}$

$$= \begin{bmatrix} aA + bB + cC & aX + bY + cZ \\ xA + yB + zC & xX + yY + zZ \end{bmatrix}$$

$3 = 3$ OK $\Rightarrow \{2 \times 3\}\{3 \times 2\} = \{2 \times 2\}$

Example #2: $\begin{bmatrix} 1 & 2 \\ -2 & -1 \end{bmatrix} \begin{bmatrix} 3 & 4 \\ -2 & 1 \end{bmatrix}$

$$= \begin{bmatrix} 3-4 & 4+2 \\ -6+2 & -8-1 \end{bmatrix} = \begin{bmatrix} -1 & 6 \\ -4 & -9 \end{bmatrix}$$

$2 = 2$ OK $\Rightarrow \{2 \times 2\}\{2 \times 2\} = \{2 \times 2\}$

2 x 2 Matrix Determinant (also known as the cross-product): $\det \begin{bmatrix} a & b \\ c & d \end{bmatrix} = \begin{vmatrix} a & b \\ c & d \end{vmatrix} = ad - bc$

3 x 3 Matrix Determinant (also known as the cross-product):

$$\det \begin{bmatrix} a & b & c \\ d & e & f \\ g & h & i \end{bmatrix} = \begin{vmatrix} a & b & c \\ d & e & f \\ g & h & i \end{vmatrix} = a \begin{vmatrix} e & f \\ h & i \end{vmatrix} - b \begin{vmatrix} d & f \\ g & i \end{vmatrix} + c \begin{vmatrix} d & e \\ g & h \end{vmatrix}$$

PROBABILITY

Constants & Variables:

E: event
P(E): probability of event
τ: number of target outcomes associated with event
T: total number of possible outcomes
r: indicates number of elements to be grouped together in subsets
n: total number of elements in set
r: indicates number of elements to be grouped together in subsets

Probability Equation:

The probability of an event occurring is the ratio of the number of target outcomes to the total number of possible outcomes.

$$P(E) = \frac{target}{total} = \frac{\tau}{T}$$

Product or Factorial Notation:

General Factorial:

$$n! = \prod_{i=1}^{n} i = i * (i + 1) * (i + 2) * \cdots * n = (1 * 2 * 3 * \ldots * n)$$

Sequence Factorial:

$$P_n = \prod_{i=1}^{n} a_i = (a_i * a_{i+1} * a_{i+2} * \ldots * a_n) = (a_1 * a_2 * a_3 * \ldots * a_n)$$

Simplifying a Fraction Factorial:

$$\frac{n!}{(n-r)!} = \frac{n(n-1)(n-2) * \cdots * \cancel{(n-r)!}}{\cancel{(n-r)!}} = n(n-1)(n-2) * \cdots * 1$$

Permutation:

Describes the number of arrangements that can be formed from "n" total elements, taken "r" elements per arrangement with a specified order.

$${}_r^n P = \frac{n!}{(n-r)!}$$

Example: Given set {A, B, C} find the number of permutations taking 3 elements per arrangement.

Set Notation: ${}_3^3 P\{A, B, C\} = \begin{Bmatrix} ABC & BAC & CAB \\ ACB & BCA & CBA \end{Bmatrix}$ No. of Permutations: ${}_3^3 P = \frac{3!}{1!} = 6$

Therefore, set {A, B, C} can be permutated 6 times taking 3 elements per arrangement.

Combination:

Describes the number of groups/combinations that can be formed from "n" total elements, taken "r" elements per group disregarding order.

$${}_r^n C = \binom{n}{r} = \frac{{}_r^n P}{r!} = \frac{n!}{r!(n-r)!}$$

Example: Given set {A, B, C} find the number of combinations taking 2 elements per group.

Set Notation: ${}_2^3 C\{A, B, C\} = \{AB \quad BC \quad AC\}$ No. of Combinations: ${}_2^3 C = \binom{3}{2} = \frac{3!}{2!1!} = 3$

Note that order is disregarded therefore {AB BC AC} ≡ {BA CB CA}. So, set {A, B, C} can be cominated 3 times taking 2 elements per group.

STATISTICS

Data: Set or sequence of numbers; ex. $\{a_i\}_{i=1}^{n} = \{a_1, a_2, a_3, \cdots, a_n\}$

Statistics: Mathematical science of analyzing data to develop probability models (an effort to discover trends in the past and apply these trends to the future).

Mean: Average or central value; sum of data divided by the number of data points.

$$\text{mean} = \frac{\text{sum}}{\text{count}} = \mu = \frac{1}{n} \sum_{i=1}^{n} a_i = \frac{S_n}{n}$$

Median: Middle number in a data set ordered least to greatest.

Frequency:	The number of times a data point occurs within a given data set.
Mode:	The number in a data set that has the greatest frequency or most common occurrence.
Range:	Difference between the largest number and smallest number.
Deviation:	The difference between each data point and the mean; $a_i - \mu$
Variance:	Average of squared deviations.

$$v = \frac{1}{n} \sum_{i=1}^{n} (a_i - \mu)^2$$

Standard Deviation:	Describes the spread of a data set which shows how much the data (as a whole) deviates from the mean; square root of the variance; $\sigma = \sqrt{v}$

Box and Whisker Plot:

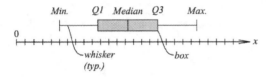

$Q1$ is the sub median between the minimum and median values and $Q3$ is the sub median between the maximum and median values.

Useful Summations for Statistics:

Summing Consecutive Numbers: $\quad S_n = a_1 + (a_1 + 1) + (a_1 + 2) + \cdots + (a_1 + n)$

Summing Consecutive Odd and Even Numbers: $\quad S_n = a_1 + (a_1 + 2) + (a_1 + 4) + \cdots + (a_1 + 2n)$

Final Remarks:

The SAT and/or ACT will not define your life. If you don't do as well as planned, that's okay. In my opinion, a large portion of kids graduating high school would benefit from going to a two year / community college afterwards rather than going directly to a four year university. You will save a large sum of money and this gives you more time to decide which direction you want to take your career in. When I was in high school, I never put much thought into my future. After graduating, I stayed home with my parents and enrolled at my local community college where a standardized test score was not required. I was fortunate enough to have parents who gave me time to figure out who I wanted to become. In college, I finally felt as if I could breathe and focus on one thing, which was school. High school consists of long days, going from class to class, then practice, then homework, day after day. College is a time to really buckle down to focus a majority of your time to learning key skills you'll need for the rest of your life. This also includes becoming familiar with learning on your own and becoming, for lack of a better word, comfortable with being uncomfortable.

My final year at community college was actually one of the best years of my life. I met people from all different backgrounds where the force of our gravitation was driven by our drive and motivation to get out of community college. After transferring, I graduated with a bachelors in science, worked two different internships between summers, then worked a full time job for approximately 3 years. I was able to pay off all my loans, save over $60,000 (which is mostly gone now) and bought a car upfront for $20,000. It wasn't long before I realized that I needed to be doing more so now I'm struggling through graduate school but at least I put myself in a position where I could financially do so. My friends from county college went off to graduate programs at Rutgers, Yale, and NYU. Others went off to work for companies such as Merck and NASA. Some went off to work at local engineering firms and startups. I also know people who dropped out of college and are now successful trades people who work very hard, do jobs that are necessary to make life possible as we know it, and are making much more money than entry level desk jobs that "require" the standard four year degree.

We are all told that we need college and that the best years of our life will be in college so what most of us do is take out tremendous loans, go away to a four year school, get the "college experience" then settle into a monotonous job where we become stuck because we are in too much debt to feel free to go out and risk another career. College is four years long. We live a lot longer than that so why put all your eggs in one basket when you're not even sure that those are the eggs you want. I quit my job two years ago because it was too easy and I had the freedom to do so. I could not live with the idea that this was going to be what I was doing for the next 10 to 15 years if I didn't make a move now. After leaving, I stumbled for a bit, then went through the craziest year of my life while working as a mathematics instructor at C2 Education in both Westfield and Bridgewater, NJ. After a couple months, I began writing these "tool sheets" for myself to have as a reference while teaching and for my students to have as a reference while working through practice tests. I kept writing and editing and eventually it became this. I hope it helps in your pursuit. Good luck and go get it.

Printed in the United States
By Bookmasters